NEW
HORIZONS

OXFORD

Secular
SATB (with divisions)
and piano

—CONNOR J. KOPPIN—
Where Everything is Music

Written for Robyn Starks Holcomb and the Sioux Falls Roosevelt Concert Choir, Sioux Falls, SD

Where Everything is Music

Jalāl ad-Dīn Muhammad Rūmī
13th-century Persian
trans. Coleman Barks with John Moyne

CONNOR J. KOPPIN

Don't wor-ry_____ a-bout sav - ing_____ these songs,__

don't wor-ry_____ a-bout sav - ing_____ these songs!__

Duration: 4.5 mins

Printed in Great Britain

OXFORD UNIVERSITY PRESS, MUSIC DEPARTMENT, GREAT CLARENDON STREET, OXFORD OX2 6DP

The strum-ming___ and the flute___ notes

The strum-ming___ and the flute___ notes___

The strum-ming___ and the flute___ notes

The strum-ming___ and the flute___ notes

___ rise,___ rise,___ rise,___

___ rise,___ rise,___ rise,___

___ rise,___ rise,___ rise,___

___ rise,___ rise,___ rise,___

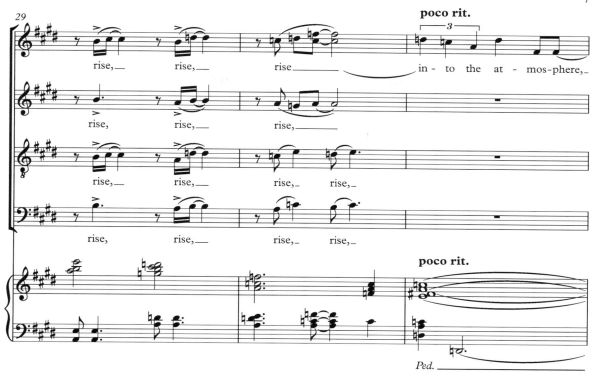

ISBN 978-0-19-352900-7

9 780193 529007